PEACE OF MIND FOR THOSE WITH EVERYTHING ON THE LINE

YOU ARE NOT
ALONE

J.D. HOUVENER

CONTENTS

FOREWORD

Who Should Read This? It is my hope that this volume makes the reading or listening lists of any of those who may consider themselves a contemporary Entrepreneur.

But who is an Entrepreneur? Exactly who do I mean by those with everything on the line? And try not to apply those stereotypes just yet—my answer may surprise you!

Maybe you have already begun a venture; or you are just now mapping it out. It could be that you have an idea and you want to find out how to bring it into the world.

Have you imagined yourself as the owner of a retail shop, offering a useful and quality product to grateful customers?

Or, perhaps you are an innovative mechanic with an idea for a new tool who wants to learn how to make money and improve technology in your field.

Regardless of your industry, you have business goals to pursue and the courage to do so. Even if you have doubts about whether or not the ideas presented in this book are for you, I urge you to continue reading. Why? Because not only do I offer encouragement based on my personal experience, but also in today's digital world, even the "starving artist" has unprecedented access to a potentially huge marketplace. Success is possible! It IS worth the inherent risks involved.

Because the internet can be an incredible equalizer (think crowd-funding vs. VCs and digital advertising space vs. billboards or newspaper and magazine ad costs and reach), more people than ever have a platform to connect and market their products and services.

That said, I believe the contemporary Entrepreneur to be much more than someone with an internet connection and a computer: I believe it is a **lifestyle**.

WHO WE ARE

We are members of a class **self-motivated** to use our skills, talents or special knowledge to create an impact and sustain a way of life on our own terms.

Passion drives us. The mindset of the innovator includes an intrinsic desire to a keep pushing forward when others would not dare. In essence, we're adventurers.

Exciting as it sounds, this way of life does not come without its particular struggles. What sets us apart also isolates us. In this way, one could say an Entrepreneur is both an independent outfit *and* a member of a subculture created by all of our collective experiences. Think you have nothing in common with a patent attorney like me? If you read on, I suspect it will become clear to you that there are values and ideals common amongst all of us who share goals and traits akin to what I've described above. That's not to say having a team isn't (in most cases) crucial support—but the opportunity to level with someone leader-to-leader meets an altogether different need.

WHY I WROTE THIS BOOK

More to the point, what I have seen is this: nearly all who set out to do something new, or create something of their own, will face similar obstacles throughout every stage of the process.

This book is an effort; a study in how to view these obstacles in ways that will help you to overcome the fears and frustrations that accompany entrepreneurship. As Amanda Austin, founder and president of **Little Shop of Miniatures** said in a recent *Business News Daily* article titled "Entrepreneurship Defined: What It Means to Be an Entrepreneur," you've got to "be able to stomach the roller coaster of emotions that comes with striking [it] out on your own." [1]

At its best, this guide is a call (for those of us who are so inclined) to contribute to a micro-level movement that, as I see it, has the potential to strengthen and improve, both individually and collectively, our economy and quality of life in conjunction with an increasingly global market and culture.

I have taught myself a set of guiding principles that have helped me navigate my way through to the vision at the end of what can seem like a long and, at times, lonely tunnel. If you are ready to hear it, I'd like to share with you how these guidelines work.

A LITTLE ABOUT ME

I realize it may be difficult for you to imagine that a patent attorney could be understanding of an entrepreneur's concerns and anxieties, or their motivations and successes. Because of this, I am going to share a little about my background.

In 2007, I graduated from the University of Washington with an Industrial and Systems Engineering degree. That same year, I went to work for Boeing.

At Boeing, I worked on the mid-body fuselage and empennage (tail) design teams for the 787 Dreamliner. At the same time, I acted as the regulatory liaison between Boeing and the FAA, managing their safety compliance issues.

Like many entrepreneurs, I am a lifelong learner. At this point in my career, I also knew that I wanted to lead a team. So, I signed up for the MBA program at Seattle University in 2010 as the first step to a management position within Boeing. However, after completing a fascinating business curriculum, I quickly learned that what I *really* wanted was to be a business owner. And although I knew an engineer was not the typical background for an entrepreneur, it was here that I discovered the key to what would be my business—and from that discovery came the creation of my law firm, **Bold Patents**.

Yes, I left Boeing because punching someone else's time clock was not how I wanted to live, but what seemed worse was the idea that my income and influence were to be dictated by someone other than myself. On that same token, I wouldn't be able to interface directly with the consumer side; to see firsthand the results of my efforts and how to continually improve business.

The path to Bold Patents was set in motion during spring of 2012. The University held a startup competition. The set up was much like the ABC show *Shark Tank*. Each competitor sat in front of a panel and was asked a series of questions from would-be investors.

Over and over again, the question about intellectual property (IP) came up. And within that framework, questions about patent law and invention ownership. It had such pull, and products or services with IP assets such appeal with the panel, I just had to know more about it.

The Road to Riches is in Niches

These words of wisdom came from my entrepreneurship professor at Seattle University. It is imperative that you discover your own niche within your business concept. Maybe it is already obvious to you and you are already honing your market strategy, but many of you may still be trying to narrow in on what niche in your chosen field fits you.

Again, this begins with embracing what you are passionate about. For example, my studies at business school lead me to believe that competitive advantage and development of reproducible systems for achieving scalability and growth are the big keys to any business. I thought long and hard about my personal skills and interests and how I might someday achieve the same success. I knew I enjoyed technology and working with other people that were excited about developing new ideas.

After looking into my various options, I discovered that a Patent Attorney is someone who has both a background in either the science or engineering fields, has completed Law School and passed the Patent Bar.

When I learned that their job is to represent inventors before the 'patent in trial' appeal board at the United States Patent and Trademark Office, I knew what I wanted to do: go to law school, become an attorney and open my own firm. But not just another firm: the idea was to combine patent protection expertise backed by a Bar license, an engineering and design background with experience *and* a degree in business. I would offer a unique, valuable service to a growing market. Thus, Bold Patents.

Though I believe an entrepreneurial spirit is an innate part of one's personality, it was my MBA curriculum that officially introduced me to the worlds of business and marketing; here that I became inspired by the sales and operations process and, at the heart of that education:

➤ **The impact of leadership,**

➤ **The value of quality products and services, and;**

➤ **My potential, both personally and professionally**

Understanding the above is an ever-evolving process, to be sure. That's why I call Entrepreneurship a lifestyle. And so, I write this book partly for myself, to reflect on what I've learned during my years so far as an entrepreneurial attorney and partly for you, as a means of support.

Of course, your business journey will almost certainly vary greatly from the path that I took. Nonetheless, my learnings are applicable to business owner's and innovators of any field.

Now you—as ones who identify as creators and entrepreneurs inevitably will do—may ask yourself: am I a part of this group? And: is this book for me?

Luckily for both of us, you do not have to decide if this mindset is right for you BEFORE you read on.

WHAT DOES ENTREPRENEURSHIP AS A LIFESTYLE MEAN?

Is This Lifestyle For You?

Does your age matter? Maybe. Perhaps someone, say, younger than 25, has not experienced enough to value the creation of a life through one's personal work. On the other hand, someone over 60 may be set in their ways, or might lack passion.

I say these things not because I am ageist, but because this is the general norm. That obviously does not preclude the precocious 80-year-old, or the mature-beyond-their-years college freshman.

The key to making it work is that you have to be ready. And in order to be ready for the program I am about to map out, you need to view your entrepreneurism as something that encompasses every major aspect of your life. (I'll wait while you take a deep breath and let that sink in a bit).

A Unified Purpose and The Bigger Picture

Simply put, this lifestyle works best when you have committed to constantly pay attention to these facets of your life and live by a system of checks and balances.

I'll get more precise in the next few pages about what this system entails, but first I want to talk about why I find adhering to a code like this is necessary to succeed.

The answer is sort of like the raindrop on a river's surface. On impact, the individual drop will affect the whole of the body of water. And in that moment, the drop also becomes an inextricable part of that whole.

And while to some this may sound overly philosophical, what I am getting at is this: the ideas in this book are best suited to those who want their impact to be made in an organized, well-planned effort that focuses on the positive development of one's environment and to the benefit of the industry one serves. The go-getter that will reap the most from the plan I am about to share understands—or more, has the desire to honor—the importance of a holistic approach to thinking, acting and therefore living.

Which Aspects, Specifically?

Well, for example, **your health**. Ideally, you are selective and thoughtful about the food you eat—or at least, this is a future personal goal.

Your Footprint. Sustainability is important to you. Using, and adapting how you function along with the evolution of technology is a part of your lifestyle—and you have an eye for the future. You are concerned with a plan to provide for yourself as well as an estate, a cause or industry and/or a family.

You want the things that matter to you to be supported by the work that you do. Let me tell you, this does not happen by accident. You must be willing to review every aspect of your life and treat it (or have a desire to treat it) as an integral part of a larger system. Of course, any system needs to be researched, established, organized, monitored and nurtured in order to function. And, in order for a system to produce optimum results, careful thought must go into the conception and craft of each of its components.

More Examples of Entrepreneurial Aspects:

➤ You like to play board or word games; even computer games. Your Type A tendencies feed your competitive spirit (even if you happen identify as more Type B— some of us do!). This book will touch on how competition can help you thrive in business _and_ in life.

➤ You research products and services before you buy.

➤ While you have a do-it-yourself spirit, you not only realize the importance of time, you're beginning to understand where your strengths are and to appreciate the value of delegation.

➤ In short, this book is a support guide for those who have the desire to be an entrepreneur. It's goal (my goal) is to help bridge creativity and independence by way of a thorough, organized plan of execution. Through the lens of your business, we address all major areas of your life.

You're Motivated! But You're Frustrated...

A leader is driven by his or her desire to make a difference; to leave a mark upon a society, a field of study or an industry. This could mean initiating a social change, revolutionizing a system or simply building a quality team to support your product or service.

A clear example of this would be Apple Inc. and Steve Jobs' influence on communication and entertainment device design. The iPod's function and construction, for instance, have changed the way we listen to music and contributed to the visual aesthetic of our global culture.

On a smaller scale, but no less valid (remember the drop of water?), would be the successful family bakery. The secret family recipe can influence the food we eat and even how we interact with our friends and families.

The "warm fuzzy" that exists, I think, for all entrepreneurs is the idea of having made a difference. What kind of difference, of course, is determined case by case. And if you're reading this book, you want to initiate real change—an evolutionary push. Most likely, that change will be something that you are personally passionate about. And you are going to want to instill this passion in not only your teammates, but also your fellow leaders, your community, and—ultimately—in your clients who pay for and benefit from your products and services.

That's Right! But, How Do I Succeed?

This is a tall order. Beyond practical and logistical frustrations, lie internal and interpersonal conflicts that MUST be dealt with. These conflicts are challenging and will require you to use insight, patience and even compassion.

Are you picturing the whole gang smiling as you excitedly map out your latest solution?

Are they nodding in enthusiastic agreement? You might want to re-think that picture in your mind's eye.

There's no easy way to say it: you're generally going to have to rely on yourself to deal with many issues. Remember, even if others in your organization share your passion for the subject matter, this is *your* baby. They looked for a leader. You chose to be that leader.

Sometimes, the actions needed, or solutions reached are ones that only we are a part of—perhaps they are ones only we believe in. But that's because we have that extra drive and passion; i.e. that entrepreneurial spirit that maybe no one else in our organization has.

The natural result of this can be a tendency to be distrustful of a colleague's intentions or skeptical that an employee will handle situations as diligently or appropriately or as possible.

You *will* get frustrated—I'd say it's impossible not to. Few people can understand the disconnect between the admiration the average person has for the entrepreneur who is or has accomplished a business goal and the skepticism, sometimes scathing criticism from that same person towards the one who has chosen to chart his own, perhaps daring, course but has yet to bring his or her ideas fully to fruition. Truly, the seasoned risk taker will face skepticism on his unproven idea even in the face of prior successes.

Let that sink in. This is not an easy or pleasant understanding. However, it is **critical** that you do your best to avoid negativity in your day-to-day interactions.

As I continue to discuss this, and other frustrations throughout the book, I will touch on some productive ways to become (and remain) proactive and optimistic, giving you the tools to move forward—even in the face of skepticism.

Frustration Number One: Dealing with Fear.

Fear covers most any category here, but the solution that will inevitably override our fear is to simply **act**. Taking charge and moving forward into your fears—even in the smallest of ways—is what eventually absolves it.

I've listed here some of the most common fears and most stressful situations we experience:

Funding. Can I Build It?

Let's face it, getting funded is (for most folks) a huge challenge. Perhaps the biggest frustrations in entrepreneurship are about finances. Honestly, this one of those frustrations that plagues us in various forms at all stages of business ownership. This hotly discussed topic will be addressed at length in this book.

You're Funded But...

Payroll. You don't know if you're going to be able to make your next payroll!

Overhead. You don't know if you're going to be able to make a payment to a vendor!

Accounts Receivable. Unlike a steady paycheck, it is not always guaranteed that you will get paid for the work that you do. You will most likely, to some extent, need to go to certain lengths outside of invoicing to collect a payment. *If* you ever collect it once it's reached this stage.

Marketing and Customer Data. This can be a major financial and operational frustration. What you think you know about consumers may not be a market reality. This can cause an expensive marketing campaign to fall flat or miss it's mark entirely. You may have to hire marketing or data professionals. Knowing how to market your product or service and to who can be an overwhelming undertaking, but it really comes from premium (and in many cases pricey) market research. However, performing this kind of informed customer profiling is essential to achieve the percentage of the market segment you project to capture.

How Do We Get Through It?

A desire to succeed is really all that's needed at the end of the day for an entrepreneur to stay inspired. No matter what anyone else says, when you're all alone, you're still ready to take what you know, review what you've learned, and pivot as needed to get the job done. This passion is what will supply you—and eventually your team—with the energy to keep moving forward.

The Importance of Impact: Be the Change

Now here you are—you've committed to do whatever you need to make your business work. You have an enduring passion to create something. You also understand, to some degree, the myriad of challenges: financial worry, building a customer or client base and maintaining this desire to succeed. However, there will be fallout from the practical reality of such frustrations.

In this next section, I talk about some of the fallout from these challenges and how one key perspective can deal with these consequences in a productive and reliable way.

Becoming Distrustful

The biggest risk to our business endeavors is that these concomitant frustrations make it easy for us to become excessively or cynically distrustful of other people—vendors, employees, your management team—so that we no longer believe they can or will do their jobs. I think a healthy skepticism is essential, but an overriding attitude of suspicion in your working relationships can cause incalculable damage. Once trust has been derailed in a work relationship, it is very difficult to get it back on track. The costs of lost time, buried ideas, information left unshared, etc. can be exponential.

Lone Wolf-ing

It then becomes easier to compound distrust with an inordinate need to control, to do everything yourself. Larry Broughton, an entrepreneur, author and former Green Beret, had this to say about the "lone wolf":

Falling for this "go it alone" fable on your entrepreneurial journey puts both your short and long-term success at risk. Following the Lone Wolf story line also virtually guarantees you will struggle harder (and longer) and waste more of your time and money on the way to success (if you make it at all). [2]

As Broughton says in his article, this attitude is brought on by an inherent do-it-yourself type attitude but can also arise from the seeming loneliness of taking on a leadership role.

Indeed, this tendency is much more than a lively sense of initiative—I am talking about an almost obsessive or compulsive need to manage every task, believing you are the best one to handle any and every job—even those outside your wheelhouse best delegated to a specialist or colleague. Keep aware of your mindsets constantly. If you are experiencing burnout, ask yourself, am I lone-wolfing?

Over-Ambition

In addition, our desire to succeed can actually hinder our growth. How? Well, this type of fallout comes from over-focusing on our wants: we **want** to have more access to people, more finances. We **want** more confidence and to feed our desire to succeed. Naturally, we **want** more customers. We **want** to make a difference. These "wants" begin to add up, and this attitude of wanting to receive and be given things can also lead to burnout and, what's more, can cause friction in our relationships and distract us from what should be our primary focus of quality and value for the service or products we provide.

So, What's This Key Antidotal Perspective?

"The first and most important choice a leader makes is the choice to serve, without which one's capacity to lead is severely limited."

-Robert Greenleaf [3]

The answer to either avoiding or coping with these pitfalls (and the path to professional satisfaction) is simple, yet following it poses some degree of a challenge for most people.

In short, it is to maintain an attitude of **leadership through service.** The path to sustainable entrepreneurship *requires* you to give your time and focused, dedicated energy to your activities and living by this mindset: that any given circumstance be approached with an attitude of "how can I best serve this situation," as opposed to the mentality "what can I get out of this situation."

It is critical to maintain this philosophy. For those of you who may think this does not sound like much fun; for those of you who this will be a transition for, I suggest you read further still and discover the ways in which you *will* gain. The benefits of such an attitude are worth the investment in a new way of thinking.

You cannot short circuit the process. In order to receive your successes, you must first put in the effort. The more effort you put in to serve your employees, vendors and customers, the more efficient and robust your business can become.

As I will repeat throughout this book, being an entrepreneur is most rewarding when you commit to it as a lifestyle.

The key here is that this approach first be adopted by you as an individual; on a personal level.

This book discusses the idea of service in all of its angles. Both active service through spirit, active service through family, your health and your work.

Read through this list of ways you can give. Think of how you can use these to start giving more in your own life.

Ways to Give:

1. **Building confidence**
2. **Training Staff**
3. **Providing access to knowledge**
4. **Recognizing and taking advantage of teaching moments**
5. **Making financial commitments**
6. **Being emotionally supportive**
7. **Being spiritually supportive**

You will begin to see fruit from the seeds of generosity and appreciation in your personal life. This attitude will then carry over organically into your business. When you focus on the quality of your product and the needs of your customer before profit, the money will take care of itself.

One of a Kind Mind

You are at this point, I hope, convinced that you either are, you will be, or you now aspire to be what I consider a contemporary entrepreneur. That's great!

We've gone over some of the frustrations common to this lifestyle, the pitfalls of over-ambition and introduced the idea of how these dangers can be dealt with through a philosophy of service. What follows in this section is a quick breakdown of the main tenets of this book.

Building Brand Awareness Starts with You

Because this philosophy is so important—and so personal—I have devised a short module for building an outline that will help you to clarify, in your own words, how you can best serve your business. You will do this by examining your reasons for building it as well as taking a closer look at what drives you and what you are passionate about. This will enable you to more effectively communicate your goals and overall vision to your team, your customers and your constituents.

The more clearly you can get them to see what you see, the more you will be able to motivate everyone else around you to move forward with their role in your business concept, product or service.

Money Matters

This module also includes a discussion on the particulars of how you make money and how to optimize your revenue. I'll ask you to identify all possible sales channels and do a competitive analysis so that you can explore how to best position yourself against your competition.

Recognizing the Learning Curve

In addition, we'll take a look at the need to continually educate yourself—a requirement for any good leader—and use that discussion to delve into what leadership means for you and your business.

At the end of each chapter, I encourage you to take a moment, reflect, add notes, and fill out the provided checklist as applicable. I know this may seem tedious to some of you, as taking similar inventories has most likely been asked of you many times in the past. Regardless, I believe this is one case in which you to owe it to yourself to take a few minutes, grab a pen or a paper (or even this book itself) and sketch out in your own handwriting, from your own mind, your high-level master plan.

That plan, obviously, is one thing I cannot specifically give you.

I can, however, tell you that, if you follow this guide, it will lead you to a path of success through service, as it has for me.

You will inevitably find, as you complete the checklists at the end of each chapter summary, that you are able to articulate your vision with increasing clarity. Truly, you need to sell this vision to yourself unreservedly before ever approaching teammates, your co-founders, members, customers, clients—anyone else!

If you are of true conviction about this passion, energy, and reason for being in business others will see it in your eyes. They'll hear it in your voice--and they'll start believing in it, too.

Once all that you've discovered, learned and changed by reading this book and completing the checklists is aligned, it will begin to coalesce with all of the other experiences and information you've gathered over the years. This knowledge can then lead you down a powerful, purposeful path.

Yes, I've been through this process. And guess what? I am *still* going through it. If you haven't already, you will soon find out that you won't go through this practice of refinement just once—being your own boss requires a continual effort to hone your focus while moving towards that singular purpose.

Let this book and this system be a guide to look to when you are struggling and find yourself deviating from your course. Then, look back on what you wrote here. You will rediscover that core drive and recognize that in pursuing this thing you are passionate about, you are giving service to a community that needs it.

That's right! We are going to talk about how *you* are **one of a kind** as a leader and an entrepreneur of your business; your product or service in the marketplace.

What you have works because you saw the need, identified how to satisfy it and then created that solution. This is indeed unique. I am here to help you make the most of your opportunities and talents.

YOU ARE A LEADER...BUT YOU ARE NOT ALONE.

"Leadership is the capacity to translate vision into reality".

—Warren Bennis [4]

A s a leader you think differently than others. You are, in the real sense, a pioneer. One who endeavors down a path without a clear map, or without necessarily the knowledge or foresight of what's to come. But with this inherent courageousness and drive, you are learning that if you face things head on, you can handle anything that steps into your path. What's more, is that you can see the forest for the trees. In other words, a future that many others cannot.

You're not focused on the rocks and dirt beneath you or even the shape of the path that winds before you. No, you envision the bird's eye view: the waterfall in the clearing; the resting place and the goal of the journey.

This approach to taking the path is not universal. In fact, most people don't think this way at all. However, we are all on the journey. Leaders exist to make sure the camp reaches the clearing. In this way, we can enjoy the recognition leaders receive. However, we must also acknowledge the responsibility associated with the job. We will be the ones to set the tone for the work, train our team, provide materials and make key decisions. It is you alone who is front and center before the wild.

Of course, as I've said, this role can feel lonely. Those on the path with you have different thoughts about how to reach the journey's end. This can be frustrating. What's to remember is that not only do they need you to move forward with their own goals, you need their personalities and talents to support your endeavor.

With every interaction, teaching or training moment keep in mind that they need your confidence to inspire and motivate them to continue to the end. The care and quality with which you do this will affect your success. Indeed, their success *is* your success. You cannot thrive without them.

You Serve First

"You first" is something I will repeat in this chapter perhaps more than anything else. Because you are the leader you need to make the first moves. In a business, often times this means creating rules and regulations; a structure under which to operate. These policies are guidelines for your employees and the way in which you set expectations for them. This might be best described as your workplace "culture" and that culture is introduced to prospective employees immediately, right at the interview stage, perhaps even at the application stage.

From the perspective of partners, shareholders or members, the first move you made is who you have become based on your experience and education. They entrust you with creating that culture or structure because of what have you learned and what you have done thus far.

To retain that trust, and cultivate it in your team, the next "first move" is one of service. Service is the most genuine form of leadership. In general, this is a willingness to share, provide and give first without an immediate expectation of a return.

Kaizen

In accordance with the structure set by your policies, are your organization's mission and operations. For your structure to remain solid, these must all be built around the idea of service--whether it be the level of service given to the customer or client or operating in a way that best serves the quality of your product.

The internal processes you create to render your products and services dictate how these products and services will be received in the marketplace. Of course, its success is also determined by how you first deliver it, but we'll dig into the sales process more specifically in later chapters.

There's a famous saying that originated in the creation of Toyota's manufacturing system. It's called "Kaizen." Translated, it means "continual improvement." [5]

Right now, I want you to simply recognize that, when you do feel alone, having a system and a process for delivering your service in a way that carries out your passion—from the raw material stage perhaps all the way to delivery of it into the customer's hands—and, that its delivery has a positive impact on their personal or business lives, becomes itself a source of support. And this is one source whose reliability you can continually improve upon. I urge you to take comfort in this concept, for it truly is a wellspring of strength.

Considering this concept allows you to see every day that you are truly not alone. In fact, it makes it impossible not to see yourself as a crucial part of a greater whole and a larger system: you are someone's solution; the pipeline that uniquely serves them what they need.

Of course, this is certainly a big responsibility! To get it right, it needs to be constantly monitored and improved upon. You have the power to create or weaken this support system. If you set these processes up with due diligence, this structure will be there to catch you when need be.

Burn the Boats

Have you heard the saying, "burn the boats?"

Imagine it: you and your army have just docked your boats on a hostile island with the intent to conquer it. If your soldiers have no means of retreat, they are going to fight infinitely harder as the possibility of sailing home is no longer a reality.

I love this metaphor. It means a lot to me because, as an entrepreneur and a business owner of a law firm, I know what it means to be "all in."

Burning your "boats," to take the island commits your entire team to victory—or at least commits them to fighting as hard as they'll ever fight in their life for you, the leader, and for themselves, the army.

Risky? Of course. But then again, that is the nature of running a business. You'll have your arsenal: your team, your product or service, your business structure, your passion and unique point of view. Make sure these weapons are strong enough to secure the win!

Again, you can be sure of their strength of impact when every aspect of your business is structured in terms of how your customer will be served.

To be sure, there are some practical boats that are probably wise to have such as insurance or an emergency fund to make sure that your health and the health of your immediate family is protected. But when it comes to business, you only want to have a plan A.

Plan A is to build and run your business well and serve the customers that you know need you. If you're trying to organize a plan B to just get by or to hedge your bets—a night job, maybe—your plan A will suffer. It needs *all* of your time and focus.

In fact, I'd go so far as to say that you will have a hard time convincing even yourself that Plan A will work, just by the fact that you are feeding Plan B. I recommend heartily for all those entrepreneurs to burn the boats, to stop working Plan B and to work Plan A all the way until you take the island.

A Continuous Education

Let's say you settled on the scope of your product or service and built your business model in alignment with your passion. You just burned your boats and squashed all Plan Bs. You're on the market.

Now, as the famous educator, speaker and author of the acclaimed *7 Habits of Highly Effective People*, Stephen Covey would say, it's time to look at how we can "sharpen the saw." [6] In other words, how can our organization maintain consistent ingenuity with a competitive edge?

In this section, we're going to talk about continuous learning as a tool to maintain and optimize your business operations and your company's priorities.

Mentorship

You personally will never know it all. And so, you need to learn how to make sure your business keeps a competitive edge and delivers high quality service and products to your clients and customers. And learning how to do this on your own is nearly impossible! Step One is to surround yourself with mentors, advisers and consultants.

Also, know that these advisors and counselors are not going to be perfect themselves. You will probably need to have more than one, or perhaps a group of many people, in order to have a robust and continual feed of different ways of thinking and additional industry knowledge as well as new information and insights on technological, social and environmental trends.

Truly, this continuous education is something you owe to not only yourself, but your teammates, and your entire organization. Your bottom line depends on your ability to remain open-minded and your willingness to be honest, open, and vulnerable. The ideas that have worked in the past may not work as well, or at all, in the future. You've got to make sure that you reshape, rethink, and redeliver your commodities in a way that will best benefit all parties for as long as they are in service.

The promotion of learning in turn creates an environment where, for example, the members of your team are willing to raise their hands and say, "I don't know." This creates the space for better communication and an opportunity to receive honest feedback—two key components in figuring out how to "sharpen the saw." A "know-it-all" attitude fosters a tendency toward deception, especially in the face of adversity. When the cards are down—and they will be more than once—that last thing you want is to be lied to by your own team.

Bear in mind all feedback should initially be taken with a grain of salt. It has to be analyzed and thought out before any kind of implementation. Ideas, thoughts and feelings about company matters should be exchanged daily but by no means should that interfere with the solidity of the structure you created.

An Awareness of Your Environment

Maintaining an awareness of industry and customer behaviors will teach you how to be not just proactive but WISELY proactive. You will become more equipped to best choose what to implement and what to discard and learn how to spot trends and avoid undue losses and expenses.

These skills are what will win the day when it comes to a thriving, scalable business that makes a positive impact on the world.

Definiteness of Purpose

Along with a philosophy of continuous learning and a running awareness of your industry and market, a "definiteness of purpose" is also fundamental to your ability to achieve. This phrase comes from Napoleon Hill, one of my favorite authors and experts on people. Hill wrote *Think and Grow Rich*, one of the most successful books on prosperity ever published.

7

I personally re-read or listen to the audio version of this book at least twice a year and the idea of "definiteness of purpose" is one of the first, major keystone elements he discusses.

His concept of "definiteness of purpose" is to define your goals as clearly as possible, bringing them to life first in your own mind and then to effectively express them to others as best you can.

While having goals in mind is a demonstrated aspect of realizing a vision, and it may sound like a cliché to say goals are important, there's more to be said about how you craft them.

Often, employees and folks that work for you are not able to see the big picture right away. To understand your vision, you'll need to provide them with lots of detail and, with enthusiasm, color in the gaps that may not be obvious to them. This is exactly what Hill proposes when he talks about a "definiteness of purpose." If there is a goal that must be shared amongst your team, if you need them to help you achieve it, you need to be able to explain what it is you want to do and why you want to do it as precisely as possible and in an engaging way.

The best way to do this is to imagine how the end result will look, identifying even the most remote specifics to keep your listener interested. For example, don't just tell your partners that you want to see your revenues double, explain what your new offices might look like once the goal is reached. What kind of furniture did you choose? How does your chair swivel or how does the desk feel under your arms? What are you wearing when you've hit the desired revenue mark? What might you be saying?

Most people don't typically identify these kinds of details when setting goals, but the point of doing so is that it forces you to define what you want more than ever. It makes the vision more real to you, which is especially helpful when you do feel alone and discouraged.

And this practice also gives you something else: gusto. It gives you the ability to convey your needs and desires for your business in a way that is fun; in a way that excites your peers and/or your team. You can even laugh and have fun with whatever you are working on! Enjoy striving for what you want and those whose help you need to make it a reality will start to want what you want. I've found defining your goals in this way is a powerful mechanism; undoubtedly one of the most powerful business tools in my toolkit.

THE HIGHEST HONOR: TO SERVE

A Philosophy of Service

This philosophy is the essential building block of what I consider to be a successful, contemporary entrepreneur. First, you must be sure you fully understand what exactly it is that you offer. Even if you sell physical goods, you are providing a service. Think: how much of a positive impact could you make with the manner and quality in which you provide these services?

I'd like to examine this idea more closely because I think it is the one idea that is the most starkly counterintuitive to some entrepreneurs and owners. And I truly believe there is no higher honor than to be entrusted to serve the organization that you've envisioned.

Let's first establish that even if you're selling a widget; even if you're selling widgets to another business before it gets sold to a consumer, you're delivering a service. Everything about that product—the performance, quality, any defects, all the materials, all the handling, how it gets to your consumer or client, the way it looks when presented, its basic functionality and how it improves or changes the life of the client or end-user—all of that is more important than the bottom line and what kind of profit you can make on that specific good.

Now you see why I say this thinking can be counterintuitive? Let me explain further what I mean.

If you sell goods, for instance, think about where you get your materials. Making sure these materials are sustainably sourced is all a part of building that solid structure we discussed in the last chapter. Your vendors are a part of your service model and affect the degree of impact that you have within your field and in the lives of those who use your service. From sourcing to possible obsolescence, you need to consider your entire business model and its trajectory from a service perspective.

For you, this mindset should become **uncompromisable**. Approaching each aspect of your business with the idea that you are looking for ways to best serve your business will save you from getting yourself locked into a cost or model that does not align with your passion, does not meet your company's needs and/or does not assure the highest quality service or product for your customer or client.

Perhaps this all sounds obvious. On paper, it reads like common sense. However, in practice—when you are under pressure and have to make immediate decisions; when uncertainty abounds, or you see something working well for someone else's bottom line, it can be easy to get confused and implement without thinking about the specific needs of your business or how to run it in a way that serves in conjunction with your passion.

What if someone tried to install to a Volkswagen engine in a Cadillac? It's just won't fit. Even though it may be a good idea at a high level, it functionally won't work. They might be able to take the entire engine apart and install it piece by piece to make it fit. Even if we then got the car running, the engine is not going to be nearly as efficient as it would be inside a VW frame. You'll find that in the same way, anything you put into action under these circumstances won't ever truly fit and your company will suffer.

Again, service is king. The highest honor you can achieve is to have the opportunity to serve your clients or customers and the world at large. Indeed, it is the theme that resonates the most throughout this entire book.

Understanding Your Best Service Through Others

Third Party Services: Where To Look, Who To Work With

Third parties are not only an inevitability, they are a necessity. If you want to achieve your business goals, you'll need to pay special attention to all of the different types of third parties around you. These organizations and individuals have the ability to influence, amplify and improve your service. They, too, will shape the market landscape and make a difference on how you choose to grow, innovate and maintain your competitive edge.

To be clear, third parties are those entities or people who are not a part of your business and do not directly benefit from it.

What I mean is that these parties are not an internal part of your business like an employee who receives direct compensation from you, such as the company you purchase your content management or project management software from.

Third parties are any professionals who you'll work closely with. You'll want to be sure to choose only those third-party organizations and individuals whose business ethic matches your own.

You may want to reach out to folks who *care* about your learning, your growth and the success of your business. These are people that maybe you went to college with or perhaps a graduate school professor—maybe even a family member! They can be from any of these groups or beyond, just as long as it is someone who doesn't rely on direct financial benefit from you and who will give their true perspective and their own best service. It is important that the people you entrust an aspect of your business to (your CPA, for example) be able to give you candid feedback on what you are doing and even perhaps your overall strategy.

You can find out if they are a good business match by taking a close look at their backgrounds and their experience. Then, critically weigh their advice and input against that experience.

This absolutely includes your entire supply chain—all the vendors and suppliers you need to produce your product or service. Take a look at anyone who provides an in between good or service and evaluate how they do business. If you have a physical product, who is distributing that product? What is their reputation and history?

Also, think beyond the direct goods or services your company offers and think about the goods and services that *complement* your goods or services. Who shares this market with you?

What do *they* do and what do *they* offer? How can you analyze your client's environment, take advantage of this knowledge (wisely and ethically, of course) and trade value with these other service providers in order amplify the customer experience?

In short, third parties are really just external support systems for your business. As I said above, they are an inevitability and have the power to influence—for better or for worse—your customer's experience. Be sure to carefully select such associates.

Understanding Your Best Service Through The Market

The S.W.O.T. Analysis

➤ **Strengths**

➤ **Weaknesses**

➤ **Opportunities**

➤ **Threats**

Performing a competitive study via a SWOT analysis with your competitors is one of the most powerful tools that I know of to keep yourself in demand. This analysis should be done quarterly. Ready to begin?

Strengths

This can be hard to quantify when looking at it from a high level, but for the purpose of this exercise, let's bring it down to numbers. Think: what are the most profitable services you offer?

Make a list of 3 to 5 of your top sellers or your most requested services from your top clients.

1. **Best #1**
2. **Best #2**
3. **Best #3**
4. **Best #4**
5. **Best #5**

Keeping the Pareto Principle in mind, highlight one (or two, depending on how many different products and services you offer) of your strongest money-makers. In a few bullet points, describe the key factors behind how this work or product is produced and why it is a top-seller. Remember, just 20% of your service offerings account for 80% of your revenue and net profit.

1. **Biggest Strength**
   a. **What process do we use?**
   b. **Who is involved?**

2. **Second Biggest Strength**
   a. **What process do we use?**
   b. **Who is involved?**

Weaknesses

Once you've established your strongest suits, an extremely valuable exercise is to look at the opposite end of that spectrum and define for yourself which of your offered deliverables perform the weakest. As such, these are most likely your least profitable products.

Create a list of three of your poorest performing products or services, or three aspects of your business in which you are the least skilled or experienced. Again, locate the key factors behind why; consider the answer quarterly and over a specified period of time, decide if these are services that should be kept or cut.

1. **Weakness #1**
   a. **What process do we use?**
   b. **Who is involved?**

2. **Weakness #2**
   a. **What process do we use?**
   b. **Who is involved?**

3. **Second Biggest Weakness**
   a. **What process do we use?**
   b. **Who is involved?**

Opportunities

Recognize opportunities in the marketplace. To do this, make a list of the news outlets, blog sites, books etc. that teach you about the latest technology in your field. Remember to be critical and learn how to discern innovation from trend.

1. **Best #1**
2. **Best #2**
3. **Best #3**
4. **Best #4**
5. **Best #5**

Once you feel like you've covered enough ground, write a quick, three-paragraph summary answering these three main questions:

1. How has technology changed?

2. How does this new technology create new opportunities to do what was not possible before it existed?

3. How can my company use this technology to keep current, efficient and more profitable?

Summary:

_____

_____

_____

Threats

Threats are any outside forces that can affect your company—events and issues behind your control. For example, political unrest in a popular tourist destination can hurt a travel agency. Accordingly, threats also include social, environmental, legislative and technological changes.

Write It Out:

1. What are some current cultural and political upheavals, new laws or technologies that might affect your industry and the way you do business?

2. How can you minimize the impact of these threats?

3. Can you ethically turn the threat around and benefit from these societal and market shifts?

4. What about your hiring practices? Are you up to date on discrimination law and Human Resource compliance issues?

Acknowledging such threats (and legal compliance issues) and operating with a constant awareness of their potential influence on your model and bottom line prepares you for any inclement weather. Burying your head in the sand will eventually get you blindsided.

SPIRITUALITY IN YOUR LIFE'S WORK

Enlightened leadership is spiritual if we understand spirituality not as some kind of religious dogma or ideology but as the domain of awareness where we experience values like truth, goodness, beauty, love and compassion, and also intuition, creativity, insight and focused attention.

—Deepak Chopra [8]

A leader must be able to follow their gut and trust their own guidance. To best serve your business (and your life), you will need to perform a certain amount of ongoing *internal* work. You cannot approach events and situations with the desire to serve an optimum positive outcome unless you seek to uphold the values quoted above in all that you do.

These values cannot be purchased; they are not materials and consist of more than just one's thoughts. In other words, they are not physical or solely mental resources. They are spiritual.

You must find a way to connect to this spiritual aspect and then connect that aspect to every facet of your business. Bring it your level of customer service, your quality of goods, the attitudes you instill in your management and the way you treat your team or employees—i.e. your entire organization and supply chain—as well as your personal life.

It is time to transcend your personal agenda and recognize the efforts of your vision will belong to a much larger network of human and spiritual interaction.

Measuring your thoughts, actions and methodology against this spiritual code will give you direction and a space to reflect. It also serves as a reminder of why you are doing what you are doing if you find yourself frustrated, feeling stuck or out of alignment with your purpose.

Is it worth the great lengths to which you have gone and will need to go to still to keep your company alive and thriving? Does it really matter that you show up every morning and cheer your team on?

When you truly understand yourself as their leader; as someone whose actions and words greatly impact those you lead, then you will understand why such a foundation is so essential and remember why you work so hard.

Exercise

Reflect: Write down one or two examples of how your actions and/or what you've said made a direct, **positive** impact on a third party, client or team member in the last month.

Analyze: How can you build on this experience and these behaviors in a way that maximizes the gain for your client/customer *and* team?

Reflect: Write down one or two examples of how your actions and/or what you've said made a direct, **negative** impact on a third party or team member in the last month.

Analyze: What did you learn from this negative outcome that will help you prevent another negative outcome of a similar situation in the future?

Enter the "Domain"

Although I am a Catholic, and the spiritual code I follow and imbue in my business is based on Christian principles, I certainly do not expect my readers to convert. I do, however, urge you to find a spirituality that makes sense to you.

That said, I am going to use the model of Jesus Christ to illustrate the essence of leadership through service. Regardless of your faith or set of beliefs, the Biblical accounts of Jesus are a superb example of how we enter that "domain of awareness."

Jesus did not gain Disciples and their fervent loyalty with threats or violence, but with an outwardly generous nature. His goal was not to secure a position of authority or to become a king, nor did he seek the approval of others.

Instead, he had the courage to put himself at the "back of the pack," if you will. A great example of this is the account of Jesus choosing to wash his disciple's feet at the Last Supper. One of the least jobs of the time was to wash the feet of traveler's who have reached their destination. In fact, this job was so menial it was delegated to a slave. With action, he illustrated how much he believed in the power of service. Instead of wielding a dictator-like authority, he was effective by serving others. While power games may work well to your advantage for a while, they do not build sustainable teams or practices. Service is a long-lasting and a proven effective form of leadership that creates strong connections—it even makes work and life more fun!

Below is a list of key ways to lead through service. Some of these we've already discussed, but they bear repeating:

1. Serve first. And don't expect immediate reciprocation.

2. Focus on the work, rather than gaining power or getting paid.

3. Use your influence over people to motivate them, not intimidate.

4. Don't use financial capability to enrich only yourself. Share; re-invest in your business as often as you can.

5. Evaluate constantly. Make sure your decisions and practices align with the values that make up your spiritual domain.

6. Continue creating. Like complacency, stagnation rots and weakens.

7. Listen and empathize with your customers and those around you. This helps you to find growth opportunities that respond directly to your customer's needs.

You will notice that I refer to these key concepts throughout the remainder of this book. Spiritual alignment is a cornerstone of this lifestyle. However, I want to reiterate that this is not a Christian text. Consequently, whether you are Christian or not, you undoubtedly can find, or know of, a similar example of leadership that resonates with these kinds of principles.

THE HEART OF SERVICE IS PASSION

And Passion means devotion. The chapters in this next section define the pillars of devotion by taking a closer look at where our passions lie and how to best align them to achieve your goals.

The Four Pillars of Devotion

Devotion is a powerful word. I think that it perfectly describes a commitment to developing your passion to lead the endeavor that is your life's purpose, to support the team that gets you where you need to be and to serve your clients faithfully.

There are four major categories of such devotion, as I see it. They are, in order of importance:

1. **Your Spirituality**
2. **Your Family/Loved Ones**
3. **Your Health**
4. **Your Hustle**

Spirituality

Nurturing the Spiritual pillar is first and foremost. This all begins with you. You set the tone and that tone will determine the fate of your success. You'll need guidance from other leaders on how to create the right environment for your business and quality of service. To do this, you need to learn from other leaders that you want to emulate. I used Jesus Christ as my example, but this role can be filled by anyone you personally deem worthy of it.

Your Family and Loved Ones

Even if you live alone, you most likely have a network or at least one other person close to you that you consider family. Your family will play a significant part in directing your business. Consideration for your family members can also help you align your goals and intentions and ultimately help you create a better value for your customer.

Your Health

The importance of this pillar is obvious in that you need to be physically present to lead and physically and mentally capable to complete tasks. You'll need energy and drive to effectively convey messages and to establish and carry forward your company's mission. In later sections, we will talk in detail about how your health impacts the way your customers receive the value of your goods or services.

Your Hustle

At the heart of the other three core pillars is your passion for business. It's that special energy and vision that you bring to the whole equation. None of this would be happening without you! Your entrepreneurial attitude pushes you to the next level and your adventurous spirit always seeks the next one after that.

Your hustle is what created the space for your employees to grow and even make a living. The services you offer (again, even if they are physical products) provide solutions for your customers. If you choose to "serve first" every step of the way, their appreciation will be well earned by you.

FAMILIAL PASSION

When it comes to one's passions, almost none speak as loud as your family. The structure of a family widely varies, but the essence is always the same: those you love who cheer you on; the ones on your most intimate team and a part of who you are. It's important to nurture your relationships with those who are your main foundation. That foundation is what keeps you solid when the loneliness of leadership creeps in.

That said, considering your company as an extension of this family goes a long way to inspire an attitude of service towards your organization. Again, there will be those who will greatly appreciate such an attitude. Your customers *will* notice this difference and award you with their loyalty.

A Desire to Provide

In terms of work and business, many are in "it" ("it" being whatever they are financially tied to) for the quick win and then dash to the next thing. That isn't what we do. We are big picture folks. Same goes for the second pillar—the second big "it" on our list—our relationships with family members.

Building a family like this successfully comes from a genuine wish to provide for whom (and to what) you have chosen to be responsible. There are many returns on this kind of long term investment, but you must be willing to plant seeds that you may not reap in your life's prime—perhaps not even in your own lifetime!

That you are building a business to sustain your family goes hand in hand with the idea that you should take care of your business the way you would your family.

Positive Reciprocation

How a family is formed and regardless of its structure, familial passion is enduring. It allows for struggle and forgiveness. Families understand that while the journey may be tough now, you are on a path to success. Again, they are on your team—even the sibling or long-time friend you haven't spoken to in six months—you can rely on them to be there in times of need for the good of the group.

You can see how this dynamic can play itself out in a company setting. An abiding approach to business relationships can evoke the same type of loyalty in one's colleagues and employees as in one's family. This is not new.

Rob Hunter, Managing Director and Founder of Hunterlodge Advertising says this [9] :

Companies with engaged employees outperform those without by more than 200 percent and en-suring team spirit and true buy-in to the company culture is a key focus for us at Hunterlodge. We have realised [sic] that recognition is an essential and key component to trust. [This is] about recog-nising [sic] our 'family' and their efforts...

Here again I must stress the idea of "you first." You will have to be the first one to extend that spirit of familial inclusion to your team. However, setting a tone of mutual trust and benefit akin to the one we ideally set with our families can pay dividends in the quality of our processes and the treatment of our customers. Those working for and with you will have to understand that there is a certain expectation of delivery. Because of the incentive of mutual benefit by maintaining that expectation, they will deliver on a consistently higher level than companies whose partners are not engaged in the long-term goals and view of the overall business scope.

The list below offers a few suggestions on how to instill this spirit of "family" in your own team. Below that is a blank list, one for you to jot down some ideas specific to your particular venture.

1. **Offer Financial Incentives for Good Work.** This offers employees a chance to put some "skin in the game." If higher work quality means higher pay, your employees will feel motivated to turn in their best—which means better output for you.

2. **Use the "Golden Rule."** It's not always easy for people to get along or treat each other

respectfully. However, if you first (there's that theme again) establish an environment built on mutual respect, your employees are MUCH more likely to follow suit.

3. **Take Responsibility.** Same idea as the Golden Rule. Showing that it is ok to admit fault will go far in gaining loyalty and sets the tone for others to do the same.

4. **Transparency.** Along with taking responsibility, giving your team a look into your goals for the company, how you operate, how the products are made, why they cost, what they do etc. instills a sense of ownership and loyalty. They become a part of building something, not simply a cog in another's wheel.

5. **Positive Reinforcement.** It's about people feeing appreciated for the work they do. Great feedback inspires more great work.

Now, think of how you can use these tools in ways specific to your own company and come up with some actionable ideas for promoting a familial culture within your team.

1.	
2.	
3.	
4.	
5.	
6.	

When employees begin to depend on one other, they also begin to hold one another accountable to the "family credo" (Mission Statement, policies, etc.). This type of work environment is far superior to a system of threats and punishments, which typically lead to deception and an ever-revolving door—both of which are extraordinarily more costly than competitive pay and bonuses or commissions to loyal employees that have earned it.

A Passion for Your Health

The third most important pillar is a devotion to your health. You'll need a healthy mind and, to at least some extent, a physically capable body to stay a solid leader. You need to be present and bring the energy, yes, but it is also about perception. As the original trail-blazer in this venture, your team needs to see that you have the fortitude and will power to do what is right for yourself. Think about it: if you cannot do what is right for yourself, how can they fully trust that you will be able to do what is right for them and for your company?

The path to fundamental mental and physical health is pretty straightforward, yet in in today's non-stop culture some of the basics bear repeating.

3 Essentials to Maintain Health:

➤ Eat fresh, wholesome foods.

➤ Curb any bad habits, i.e. no excessive smoking or drinking.

➤ Take breaks to re-charge! Take mental breaks daily and spend time away from the office.

Following these simple steps are ultimately going to make the difference in maintaining the high energy that is required to run a company successfully.

Eat sensible portions and move your body! You will be more comfortable at a healthy weight. This will also help with your mental health as well—the stress of physical ailments can be tremendous. Laboring under a potential illness can negatively impact your ability to lead and thus your team's ability to perform and your company's bottom line.

Taking a bold stance on your health transcends what you look like and sends yet another message of sustainability and long-term investment in what you are doing to your team, shareholders, partners and customers alike. In addition, those around may also focus on their own health, their own ability to perform and their personal contribution to your bottom line.

While of course health is not the primary factor in your success, there is a strong correlation between a healthy, happy and peaceful workforce and a healthy bottom line.

Doing Business

While "passion" as I've discussed it in the last three chapters can be somewhat of an abstract idea connected to your business via your spirituality, family and health, let's now get down to what is seen as a more traditional type of passion for the entrepreneur: your "hustle," that is, your work and how you execute it. Here, I will again encourage you to take a rigorous quality assessment of your business itself, of the products and/or services that you provide to your customers and take stock of your client's entire experience with your company.

As I said before, this begins with the first impression—a visit to your website, a glimpse of your logo—all the way to end of the business life cycle when they have finished using your product or no longer need your service.

Your client can only have a truly exceptional experience when you are fully engaged in your hustle, meaning that you have a deep love of your work and how you produce it. This answer may seem almost laughable in its simplicity, but this love is what will allow you and your work to excel when other modes of marketing may not. It will carry you through the rough quarters and is what will keep your focus when, during these times, something that is *not* aligned with your passion might start to look like a good idea and distract you from your true purpose.

Does that sound cheesy? Maybe to some, but so what? The truth is your customers don't think so. In fact, being passionate about your products and services and how they are delivered is what will set you apart from the competition in their minds.

Being the best in your class should always be a pursuit. Competing on price and being cheap never serves in the long run. Making sure that what you deliver is something that you yourself would want, is the best quality assurance test. Remember the perception of the Golden Rule when dealing with employees? Applying it to your products and customer care works in much the same way.

What never fails to ring true to customers is when your business produces the kind of quality and service you expect for yourself. Likewise, nothing else can impact your bottom line more positively than when customers and third parties resonate with this ethic. They'll tell other potential customers; they'll talk about it publicly in reviews and this information can find its way into all kinds of media. Your employees get the word out when they tell their friends about what they do at work and it's those third parties that carry and disseminate that glowing impression of your products or services.

A Passion For Financial Security

Perhaps a better term for this type of "passion" is financial wherewithal. I say this because some may take the desire for an abundance of money as greed or as a potentially self-absorbed idea that is not inline with a focus on service. But I totally disagree.

The goal of financial security is one that is aligned with that of ensuring that your business can thrive. Not to mention one that allows you to reap some of the benefits of taking risks and of hard work—of putting everything on the line to see your vision carried out.

In addition, this financial success ideally has a domino effect. Those you are leading should pick up on the example you set and thereby choose to work harder for you and your organization to create their own wealth.

This is by no means to say that money solves every problem—far from it. Nor is it the underlying reason to perform at the highest levels, but it certainly provides as a strong, ancillary incentive.

The point is what the money can provide that is the true benefit. This chapter aims to elucidate the benefits that can come of such financial resources.

For example, financial security can bring a better quality of life. Freedom, comfort, sustainability, relaxation and the ability to be able to get what you need (and some of the things that you want) are what also allow you to run your business optimally and be free to serve your team, your customers and your clients.

Do not underestimate the importance of this concept! Keeping an eye on maintaining your personal and professional financial security is what drives the operation of a healthy business as opposed to a self-serving search for the next sale or what might increase revenue. In other words, you need to keep a bottom line focus as opposed to a top-line obsession.

This means paying attention to ensure that your business can carry forward profitably into the next quarter, year and even decade. Remember, it all comes out in the wash. For you as the business owner to ultimately succeed, your business must first succeed.

A firm grasp on each aspect of any of your company's financial reports is critical to your overall decision-making. That said, surround yourself with trusted third parties and even direct employees who are experts, especially if you are not naturally attuned to understanding money matters.

The major aspects include (but may not be limited to):

➤ **Cash flow**

➤ **Balance Statements**

➤ **Income Sheets**

➤ **High Level Tax Knowledge**

As a leader, you must have a passion for making your venture financially successful. It's one of five facets of moving forward alongside a passion for the spiritual, for family, health and the work itself. It's *that* important.

Social Passion

"Fun is one of the most important—and underrated—ingredients in any successful venture."

—Sir Richard Branson

The Importance of Social Interaction and Sharing Passion a for it with Your Team

Having a passion for interacting socially with your team, as well as promoting (to some degree) that your team socialize amongst themselves is a great reminder of why you chose to run your own business.

If we're being honest, a big part of the reason we go into business for ourselves is to at some point be able to freely choose when and what we'd like to do *outside* of the office. Maintaining a healthy passion for fun, celebration and socialization is also a big motivator to succeed—not just for you, but for everyone in your organization.

Traditionally, leaders are taught to hold back when it comes to condoning socialization in the workplace, but I believe—and have seen—that, in fact, allowing for some social contact inspires a valuable chemistry between your partners, shareholders, employees and owners.

There are several benefits to being open about social behavior at work:

➤ It reiterates a sense of "family." As I've said before in this book, creating a familial atmosphere within your organization keeps people loyal to you as well as each other, making it more likely that they will stick it out through any difficult times.

➤ It helps you, as a leader, set the stage for balance. There will certainly be rough times or times when the workload is more than expected. If your team senses that you are in favor of social comradery and do not shun non-work discussions, this will add value to the job itself and can bolster employee retention and therefore positively impact your bottom line.

This kind of passion can direct the spirit of a company. It's this spirit that will help keep your hard-working employees from becoming weary and down-trodden during hard times when they've got to continue to keep their nose to the grindstone. In the back of their mind, they have come to expect some fun and they know they've got a boss who is not afraid to extend themselves enough to get personal about his or her own passions along with everyone else.

WHO YOU SERVE

Your Customer, Your Best Friend

You know them so well, you often know what they are going to say before they even speak. You know where they are going to be before they've announced where they plan to go. Of course, I am referring to your best friend. Whether this person is your spouse, long-time friend or grade school ally, almost everyone can relate with this type of relationship.

This kind of in-depth knowledge about what motivates a person and how that person lives is a good parallel as to how well you should know your customers—both active and passive.

With all this talk about service, we need to talk about *who* it is that your business is serving. It's no secret that an understanding of your market specs is not only crucial but also complex and hard-won knowledge. However, beyond studies and statistics are actual people. You need to get to know the people who come to you for a solution. You need to think of them as individuals and as human as you can imagine.

To truly ingrain in your mind the unique behavior and needs of your target client, we are going to create an avatar—a representation of your customer that is as realistic as possible.

On its own, this chapter is a high-level thought experiment, but the worksheet will allow you to very distinctly conceptualize who it is that you serve. Therefore, completing it is highly recommended to make the most of this chapter.

Make sure you go right now and bookmark that section, then come back here to this chapter, as it will help you complete the worksheet.

Indeed, this chapter and associated worksheet is all about the details. All the way down to what your customer looks like. We're even going to give them a fictitious name! And, remember, staying as true to reality as possible is important. If you haven't done enough market research, this exercise will make that apparent. This avatar needs to be thoughtfully crafted; to be effective, it must be a realistic representative of someone who might actually live in our society and be a part of your market segment.

These next sections go in depth on how you will get to know this avatar, as well as what characteristics to look for, keeping in mind that they may change over time. After getting to know our target clients, we will explore the best ways to deliver value both in general and for this particular customer segment.

Once we get an idea of who our base is (or will be) and how to create value for them, I will go over the importance and the worth of their loyalty. Think reviews and word of mouth marketing. Referrals are a huge part of garnering new business and what your current customers say about you can make or break your year—or even your company.

We will go over all of this in six sections to complete the study with a look at how to deliver even more value and how to turn this avatar into an advocate for your company, bringing their friends and family into your fold, so to speak.

Who You Serve—A Comprehensive Profile

The Customer Avatar

These days, you can get access to an unbelievable amount of detailed information about potential market segments. I'll repeat: getting to know as much about your client base as possible is the key to understanding how to align your business with their demands and grow along with their needs and with shifting technological and cultural environments.

To know your customer segment this well means creating an extremely comprehensive avatar. Write out—even draw out—their description using the worksheets I provided; use the space in the notes to have fun with it!

While you may have different customer segments, pick your most prominent first. Focus on one at a time.

Let's do an example avatar so that you get the idea of just how much you can learn and know about the people who use your service or buy your product.

"Suzie"

In this fictional case, your most prominent customer is a 39-year-old Caucasian woman named Suzie.

When we build Suzie's profile, we are going to tease out subtle details that may seem inconsequential but can actually affect the impact of your marketing. Really!

Her hair color and style, as a quick example, can give you insights into her priorities, the way she views herself and so on. All of these details can give you access to your customers' needs in unexpected, yet pivotal ways.

What else do we want to know about Suzie? Here are some of the initial questions you should ask yourself about her:

➤ Is she a mother? What ages are her kids?

➤ Is she married?

➤ What about her work? Is she a business owner, a stay-at-home mom?

➤ Her interests and activities. Is she involved in sports? Yoga? Painting?

➤ Her values: Politics? Charities? Facebook groups? What does she really care about? Is she of a religious leaning?

Even when you've done your research and are still not quite sure what the best answer might be, write down what your gut instinct tells you.

If you Build It...

Now that we've done some research and gathered a little information about Suzie, let's piece her story together.

What we've discovered about Suzie is that she is a single mother. She is divorced, and her kids span the ages of four through 12. She has recently moved to a new state and cares deeply for her children's education and how they're adapting socially to the new geography and the new school districts.

If you are in new home sales, or if, say, you are in the business of protecting people's liability through insurance, it is easy to see how understanding these specifics of Suzie's life can help you better serve her needs and therefore create more success for your business.

Remember how I told you that we need to know Suzie as well as our best friend? It's time to dig a little deeper.

Through various channels, we find out that Suzie is dating, although, because of her kids and her recent divorce, she is trying to keep it quiet. She uses a babysitter, maybe a local childcare service, so that she can visit hotspots on these dates. She also has a few places she likes to frequent to escape and "get away from the world."

How about her downtime? She might not have much to spare, but perhaps we learn she enjoys Netflix or Amazon Prime or even what specific shows she watches. Because she is a mom, she's using these accounts between the hours of 8:00 and 10:00 PM, when the kids finally go to sleep.

These small details might seem like minutia and not relevant to your business model, but getting to know someone at this level is a key way to learn how to target and cultivate relationships with your customers.

Sometimes completing this target customer breakdown can have unforeseen effects. You may take a step back and realize that perhaps you are at cross purposes with your market segment. This can be an unnerving experience!

As I have said many times throughout this book, the goal is to have your business be in alignment with your passions. This alignment is what makes it all work. Operating your business from a place of passion is what's going to fire you up and get you in the office on those tired Tuesdays—at least for many business owners—this drive does not come from simply the prospect of making money!

Let's stick with the insurance company example.

If you find out that, for instance, Suzie is not someone you'd necessarily want to befriend, or someone you even might like, it is possible to reposition your thinking.

What I mean is this: as I've been saying all along, your true goal is to make a difference by offering customers a service that will improve their life. In this case, you can think of the larger picture in terms of providing Suzie with security and comfort by protecting her liabilities through her insurance policy. In viewing the business relationship this way, you can create the congruency between your hopes and dreams and hers—without having to fundamentally "like" her.

In the next chapter we will continue to explore other ways to use the avatar to determine how to get down to brass tacks and actually deliver value.

Forging Customer Relationships

Now that we know a lot more about who we are serving, it's time to look at how to become increasingly valuable to them. This is obviously a strategy for longevity. The objective here is to create a constant and ever-increasing value to this customer. This kind of value plays a major role in keeping these people loyal to your company. With so much more marketing space available in the digital age, gaining loyalty should, in my opinion, be more prioritized that it already is among conscientious business owners.

Because you can now look at the avatar you created for your largest customer segment, it is possible to study and learn what they might be experiencing throughout the day. With social media, web analytics and other tools, one can discern what messaging and marketing they may already be interacting with—or even what other segments of people. From this information, it is your job to determine—and determine well—how you can deliver value. You will need to able to decide what kind of value you are capable and poised to deliver. Also, how much more valuable can you and your business become to your best friend over your competitors?

No Pressure, Right?

The answer to determining your value will get clearer and clearer the better you know your best friend. So, if we follow through on creating our customer avatar, we are also making sure that we do our due diligence for our company, for those who make up our company and, of course, for ourselves and our families.

The more thought and research that goes into the avatar, means the more informed our opinions and decisions can be.

A Worthwhile Investment

Like that of a best friend, the relationship with your customers needs to be maintained.

Pay attention to what they want! That seems logical enough, but companies not listening to their customers is actually a common occurrence—and the results can be fatal.

Take Kodak's refusal to acknowledge the growing digital camera market, for example. While competitors transitioned into the sale of digital cameras, they rebuffed demand and it cost them dearly. Worth 20 billion in 1992, the company's stock went from $94 per share in 1997 down to 65 cents each in 2011, when it filed for bankruptcy. [10]

Listening to your customers gives you access to their goals, aspirations, issues and concerns and, within that knowledge, is all you need to streamline delivery—further solidifying their likelihood of doing business again. Customized value is possible like never before—and it is worth the time spent on analyzing how you can provide it.

What are their Goals?

The relevance of determining a few of Suzie's personal goals may not be immediately apparent—but these goals can absolutely be beneficial to understand.

How? Well, if you know Suzie tries to eat healthy and is constantly on a diet, she is making a valiant effort to try and keep off a few extra pounds. She may search for various weight-loss solutions. While it may be a less than obvious angle, as an insurance company, this information may benefit you.

One way you can make use of this information is through customized campaigns. If Suzie is on your contact list, you can use such a campaign as an opportunity to build a rapport and increase your customer retention.

Maybe she has a one-year policy with you. By sending her a quarterly form or quiz checking in on her health and offering suggestions related to her goals, Suzie has a convenient way to track and improve her health. If she follows through and boosts her overall health, you can encourage her to see her doctor just before her plan is set to renew on the basis that her risk score can be reevaluated in order to lower her policy rates.

This type of exchange with your customer can be successful on a number of levels. The most obvious, beyond offering her a chance to better herself and experience life more fully, is that it builds loyalty.

Loyalty through active and thoughtful relationship building keeps those premiums coming in—and when you attract and keep a devoted client, they, as a friend would do, tell their friends and their family all about your firm and your company: how you actually care (because you really do) and their confidence in you because of a shared purpose and mission.

You know exactly what they want. You know what their needs are and anticipate them.

To further this point, the more you see entrepreneurism as your lifestyle, the more they will begin to see your company as a part of theirs. Because you can embrace your identity as an entrepreneur in every facet of life, you can become better equipped to approach your customers on a personal level, evoking that valuable loyalty.

A note about how to adapt this model...

In actuality, all we are selling in this example is a path to more self-confidence. You can approach this subject from almost ANY angle, regardless of what your goods and services are. The key is to present your product as an integral part of a larger set of solutions for a complete life and use it to point customers in a direction they already want to go; a direction that also benefits you.

Relationship Maintenance

Of course, as in anything worth obtaining, it going to take work. Loyalty comes not in an instant. Likewise, by definition, loyalty is not something that is fleeting.

Hopefully (and especially, as an entrepreneur) the promise of work does not alarm you. If handled correctly, the work needed to capture loyalty lessens over time. However, it will take a strong commitment to deliver a consistent value.

Fortunately, in the last chapter and exercise, we've already discussed one way to create value when we outlined the benefits of working towards getting to know your customer as you do a best friend. Once you reach this level of understanding, and treat this exchange as you would a friendship, value is present by nature.

Bringing It All Together

The endgame to the avatar exercise is to gain a loyal customer. A customer who will not only do repeat business with your company, but one who will be an advocate.

Advocates can be such a vital resource. They are the ones you can go to for honest feedback—again, the kind of feedback that maybe only a best friend (our favorite term!) would be able to provide. They are also someone you might eventually be able to approach for any beta testing. This type of feedback and insight from people with this level of investment in you will prove extraordinarily valuable for the successful development of your business and worth every ounce of effort.

Indeed, many loyal customers are themselves working to develop their families or businesses, in turn developing their own personal sphere of influence that can become an incredibly powerful network for you. By building up value over time consistently, the better chance you have to tap into this network.

Keep Them Coming Back

In these times of data overload and the ever-increasing ability for an organization to have continuous contact with consumers, maintaining loyalty is a bigger challenge now more than ever.

So, how does one properly manage a loyal customer, and what's the best way to continue serving a loyal customer?

Let's start by examining the biggest pitfall. The biggest mistake that companies make is to get complacent with their most loyal clientele. While they may continue to offer excellent service, they will continue to serve them as they would any other customer and expect them to remain loyal—or as loyal—for an indefinite amount of time.

Dealing with your most steadfast clients like this equals a huge opportunity missed. To wit, a loyal customer should actually be served at a higher level than any other customer or client.

This is again where the best friend analogy comes in to play. As such, they deserve to get the inside scoop, the special deals, the early releases, the ability to return a product, or even test a product at no cost, etc.

Making these kinds of benefits and features available to your most allegiant patrons is what is going make your company an integral part of their lives. Once you hit this status, they'll be on the edge of their proverbial seat waiting for your next announcement or offer. They'll also be the first to follow the launch of and purchase new product lines.

You see, once you've got a loyal client or customer, you already have a known buyer for any future product or service that you're going to sell. Beyond the obvious benefit of an existing base, extending special perks to this base will actually *save* you money in the long run. A LOT of money.

According to a study published by writer and consultant Amy Gallo in the *Harvard Business Review*, depending on what industry you are in, "acquiring a new customer is anywhere from five to 25 times more expensive than retaining an existing one." [11]

That figure bears repeating: five to 25 times more expensive! Wow!

What's more, repeat customers spend an average of 67% more than new customers! [12]

But let's dig into this a little more deeply. It's important not to fall into the trap of thinking that your current service level and/or the quality of your products or services is good enough to keep these customers loyal for as long as you are in business.

Funny enough, it doesn't all boil down to the actual product either. This kind of commitment from customers is in large part based on the reputation of your brand.

To give you a quick overview, a blog by Invesp backed by Neilsen stats, says that 59% of shoppers buy new products according to brand. In addition, marketing and customer service speaker Jay Bayer reports that a whopping **ninety-two percent** of consumers trust word of mouth and user generated content (UGC) more than traditional advertising. [13] Remember what I said about how your customers are, on some level, working to create their own sphere of influence? This statistic shows you just how crucial it is for you to earn (and then maintain) a place within that sphere—and that that happens by continuously upping your game and offering your brand loyalists significant consideration.

The Value of Public Feedback

Reviews and Social Media

So, now you've got the loyal customer. This client is your best friend. This client is someone that you've delivered value for again and again. They love you. They have become loyal. They are your ideal client, customer—maybe they have even become your actual friend! Now it's time to find more of them, because who doesn't want to share the love?

The question here is: how do you do that? How do you find your loyal client and advocate? How do you find out where they all hang out? How do you find out where more of those clients are?

Since the advent of the internet, the website and total online presence of a company is truly the 21st century storefront. This in and of itself is not new information, however, it is important to fully understand in what ways your online presence can drive sales.

I introduced a new acronym in the last section, UGC, which stands for "User Generated Content." There are two main avenues for this type of content: reviews and social media.

There are a number of sites that have demonstrated over time that they can deliver, to the best of their ability, unbiased, real reviews. Some of the big ones are of course, Google, Yelp and Trip Advisor.

As I previously pointed out citing Jay Bayer's study, prospective clients looking to assess a new business to meet a need will rely almost entirely on the reviews of third parties, as opposed to reading any of the copy, marketing, or promotional materials published by the goods or service owner. Today's consumer is a savvy one. They understand that, while your website may contain a great deal of information, this information is essentially biased toward your company and your product. They understand that you wrote that material with the intent of driving sales. Hence, they know that the best source of quality and credible information is through the reviews on a reputable site.

One of the best ways to then attract new clients to the website you no-doubt spent thousands of dollars and hundreds of hours building, is to provide such an extraordinary experience to your existing customers that they are compelled to leave you a glowing testimonial.

We've all had that experience, right? An experience with a company's employee and/or product that was so superb we just had to share it. It feels good to share these experiences and your customer's will feel the same if they receive this kind of service (there's that word again!) from you.

Written testimonials are probably the most common, but you may want to see if the client is willing to share an audio—or even better—a video testimonial. Putting a real voice and especially a face with a name to your customer's words communicates your value better than you ever could because these words are coming from a consumer in the real world. They're speaking the client's (or potential client's) language and come from this perspective, reaching others in a way you cannot.

I say this because, while you can endeavor to speak the language of your client, you'll never quite get there—but your loyal customers can get as close to understanding and conveying the position of the potential client.

Using testimonials will do a number of things for you, best of which is to allow your loyal clients to paint for you a picture of your future clients, gaining you insights you would not be able to achieve on your own.

Testimonials do this in the following ways:

1. Boost traffic to your website, which will

2. Boost confidence in your team and show you

3. New leads that give you insights as to who your demographic is and what they want.

Becoming a Part of their Inner Circle

Referrals

Once you've reached the point of obtaining customers and have had an opportunity to serve them with value, they become loyal. They're now an advocate for you, not only in their actions by remaining your customer, but by placing reviews and giving testimonial as to the quality and level of service for the goods or services that you provide.

Now comes the "golden fleece" of customer loyalty: the referral. Not only are they shouting from the mountain tops with their reviews that they love your goods and services, but they're actually introducing friends, family, and colleagues to you. Going out of their way to talk about what you've done for them; taking time from their day to push and influence others to become clients of yours. Customers of yours. This is the best of all worlds. This is what will happen if you do what I've described and gotten to know your customer like a best friend.

Just don't forget to keep raising the bar on how you deliver for them! That is how you will maintain their loyalty.

Of course, not all loyal, reviewing clients will automatically refer business to you. Likely these folks are similar to you in that they themselves are high performers. These folks may have their own businesses and they've got their own responsibilities with limited time. So, without a platform to do so, or the impetus to introduce people to you and refer business to you, it may simply not be on their minds.

But that is no reason to ignore this treasure-trove of customer response. As a business owner, you've got to be proactive and create a process to seek introductions and referrals from these types of clients. So, in the case of this segment of happy, loyal and smiling advocates, you need to *ask* for them.

The best results to this approach come from presenting a specific process for them to deliver referrals to you. So, in an email or newsletter, in person—or whichever way you contact them— be sure to include a form of some type (these days you can create forms using many of the leading marketing and outreach platforms. Think Mailchimp, ConvertKit, Google forms, etc.) so that they have a method, right then and there, to give you the information.

Although it may be uncomfortable for some of you, asking is a necessity, and the timing is critical. The best times to request a referral is when you are giving something back to them—an update on their project, a monthly or quarterly report and so on.

It should go without saying but be sure to be ultra-polite. And above all else, be sure to say, "thank you."

Be authentic and use your voice—again as if reaching out to your best friend. If you are unsure of what language you want to use, you can use the following script as a starting point:

"Hello, Mr. Smith:

I hope this note finds you well! I wanted to take a moment to let you know just how much your kind words mean to our team. We pride ourselves on our good work and are beyond thrilled that we were able to deliver top-notch [products/services] for you!

That said, the only way that we're going to be able to grow this business and continue to provide such thoughtful service/quality products is by word of mouth referrals from top clients like you, Mr. Smith. And so, it would mean a lot to us if, whether in your work or in passing, you might consider introducing us to those individuals or businesses that we can help serve as we've done for you.

With that in mind, would you please take a moment to suggest the names of three individuals that you know that aren't currently [being serviced through the industry solution we offer] who you think might benefit from our work."

Don't feel bad about putting them on the spot. These folks want you to succeed. *They* want your goods and services and so it's logical for them to want to help their friends, family and colleagues get the same superb goods and services they got. Just remember that it is important to give them structure and guidance when you do.

WHERE YOU SERVE

Point of Sale

Physical Sales

This one is fun. In this experiment, we get to delve into your customer's mind, imagine their life and try to discover what it is they actually see and touch throughout their day.

Physical sales, for the purposes of this chapter, refers to the idea that we can use one or all of our five senses to interact with the sales process in the real world. If your business is one that distributes physical, tangible products to brick and mortar stores, this discussion will probably seem most relevant to you, but many of the same principles come into play—albeit in different ways—in online sales as well.

Typically, a physical sale, by definition, is the process whereby a customer gets in their car, or hops on public transportation and travels to a store, picks a product up off the shelf, buys it and takes it home with them.

This chapter looks at how this process is a great illustration of how to conceptualize "where you serve" and expands the scope of the physical sale to match a service-based or online business model.

The way we are going to do that is by examining the life cycle of that sale beginning with the actual location where the sale will take place. Before thinking about packaging, the location of a product within that store or what (or which company's) products appear on the shelf next to it, we need to get a feel for the regions and outlets within those regions where the customer first encounters the physical product.

Some get so bogged down in the sales process that, to use an apt cliché, they can't see the forest for the trees. This is a big misstep. With all of the work you've done to learn what your customer demographic is, it would be quite the oversight to downplay the importance of the geographic regions in which they live and shop. This means that before creating and executing a sales process, you must first research and decide upon the best possible retail outlet(s) for your product. If you're selling an organic cold-pressed juice or expensive specialty cheeses, you won't want to focus on regions where there are no specialty grocers and most people in the area shop at Wal-Mart or Dollar General.

Admittedly, that is perhaps an obvious example, but it effectively demonstrates the idea: your products need to be available in regions that are in accordance with your customer profile. It is crucial to vet the outlet and retail chains and the quality of service they provide to make sure that their values align with your company image and the goals you set to serve your clients.

As we continue this study, we are going to be discussing the life cycle of that sale. We're going to be looking at the early physical manifestations of that sale, and then post-sale behavior, which is still part of the sale itself.

Beyond the Check Out

Of course, the point of sale flow is essential. There are numerous books devoted to the packaging, merchandising and pricing of goods—this is not a book on those things. To be clear, I am here to make sure that you are cognizant of those components, but the scope of this book is about how to steer the ship—not scrub the deck, so to speak.

I am more interested in creating a product to be delivered and the experience the customer has once the transaction has occurred. Make no mistake, the "sale" is by no means over at this point.

In fact, the sale is perhaps just the beginning. In my view, eighty percent of the entire transaction happens once the customer takes the product home. I say this because more often than not, customers will use and then review a product within the first 24 hours.

They purchased said product because they have a direct or perceived need for it. In general, they are excited about it and want to take advantage of their new solution right away. And when they do, they immediately rank and qualify it against any other similar products they've used.

Eight out of ten times, the reaction is mundane: "it met my needs" or "it did the job but didn't necessarily blow my skirt up"—that kind of thing. The other two times, however, a customer will either a) love it or b) hate it.

If they hate the product, they are going to yell from the mountain tops. If they love it, they will also yell it from the mountain tops—but they will in turn become an advocate for the company that produced it. They'll recommend it to their friends or online peers, and those people will recommend it to *their* friends and peers. This creates that invaluable mantle we call brand reputation. The goal here is to become recognized as an industry standout. *This* is the key part of the transactional state you should truly be cultivating.

Services

Let's circle back and talk a bit about service-based business models. I hope you folks didn't tune out because a lot of the same principles apply.

Although a service transaction doesn't involve a physical product, the manifestation of the sale is very much like that of a physical sale. In the same way a customer decides to visit and enter a store, a service customer will likewise be attracted to a certain type of quality and manner that a store front, shopping mall or even a parking lot conveys. In essence, the presentation of your business must also, as much as possible, be in accordance with your target customer profile.

You'll have to think very carefully about what they might want to see and do your research on how to position your storefront—whether it is a physical office or a website—where they might already be working, recreating or doing other business.

If you run a bail bondsman business, you rent a space near a courthouse. If you are a marketing firm, you might run ads on a site that sells business cards.

Similarly, wherever your service sale occurs, there is a salesperson that guides your customer through the sales process, just as with the sale of a physical product. You are also providing a solution to a problem, a need. Once a SOW or contract is signed and money has changed hands, the work begins. But again, like a physical sale, the major part of this transaction is the delivery of a high-quality return on your promise so that you too will create a vocal advocate.

Geography and Demographics

Let's take the United States for example. There is a lot to consider just based on US sales alone. Whether you are offering your products or services nationwide or only statewide, it's important to be aware of the available sales channels. There are two layers to be considered when thinking about geography and your business.

1. Where you are serving.

2. What channels you serve through within that geographic location.

We'll start with who you are currently serving in the present and then expand to who you would like to serve. As an entrepreneur, you've got to be a visionary. You must plan on the future of your business; where your company is going. Within that, you need to identify what changes you need to make or development strategies you need to pursue to grow or, at the very least, evolve with respect to cultural, technological and socio-economic (i.e. external) shifts.

Bear in mind your industry specific restrictions. There may be legal, ethical or other types of constraints that prevent you from going beyond certain boundaries. If you practice law, you're limited to your state jurisdiction. If you are an insurance company, there are certain licensure or certification requirements that limit the geographic bounds of your business practice. I'm not saying there are not ways around some of those limits, but there are cases where these things truly are a fixed border.

If you are operating within strict geographic limits, think about how to grow within those limits. This may sound obvious, but the path to execution isn't always readily apparent and your best approach for expansion may not always include the same processes that your current operation employs.

For example, if you've got one location on the south side of a city and serve clients in that south end, the same tactics may not work to successfully maintain a presence in the north end. Again, the key is to be mindful about who it is that you are serving.

Think of a city like Los Angeles. Any Los Angeles based business would need to align with a much different demographic in Beverly Hills than that of East Hollywood—and those neighborhoods are just seven miles apart!

Even within the same city, the presentation and marketing of your products on one end of town may not work on the opposite end. That may seem obvious, yes, but in the midst of all of your logistical, production and personnel concerns, it can be easy to lose sight of the fact that what you are offering and the way you market it needs to cater to the demographic in your location.

In addition to this, how your product is presented in the specific retail space you will sell it at within that geographic location is another big consideration. Will your merchandising plan work the same way at Big Box Retail Store A as it would Mall Kiosk B? Also, how will your packaging resemble, or contrast with, other similar or similarly situated products?

The desire to expand your business will force you to scale up (or down) the scope of your answers to these questions. If you're selling in New York city today, and your plan is to potentially grow and serve clients in Jasper, Wyoming in two years, all of your marketing answers will be different—and likely more complex--even though the products are the same. You can look to package products differently, even brand them differently and certainly display, sell, group and ship to new markets and still be able to get your products into the hands of those consumers that we've already talked about.

We've done the work to find out who they are; who your market segment is, but the entire span of folks who are seeking the solution you provide may actually live in vastly different regions and belong to many different subcultures—or completely different societies, if selling internationally. Even within different parts of the US, you and your team will need to research and assess the economic, political and social inputs in those geographic areas and how those factors might impact your business.

As a somewhat simple example, think of regional cuisine. If you run a gourmet burger restaurant chain, and you have locations in New Mexico, it would make sense to offer hatch chilies as a topping choice. You may not, however, decide to invest in serving these types of chilies at your Delaware or Maine locations.

You know your customers want gourmet burgers, but to meter and change the offerings based where these customers are geographically will optimize consumer response.

This is part of the reason why earlier in the book I said that it is important to understand your end game. If you are operating in the south side of town, to use an earlier example, and you've planned to expand to the north side of town within five years, you need to start assessing how any different geographic factors between the two sides of town might affect the way you move your product at the two- or three-year mark. Without an end game, you cannot effectively structure your company for the future. That is not to say that the plan cannot or will not need to be adjusted—most likely plans will, in fact, shift. It's that you will have an eye on the horizon and a give yourself a heads up to best situate yourself for a greater chance at successful outcomes.

Digital Point of Sale

Online Sales

The transformation of the sale from a physical world to a digital one has drastically changed business over the past fifty years. We've seen internet access that was once restricted to the elite and the affluent become increasingly available to almost every economic class. Today, nearly every consumer has at least purchased—if not also sold—goods online.

As a result, competition is stiff—and more so each year. Because of this, I want to take a chapter to talk about how niche and need are more critical than ever to capture a market.

To gain a better understanding, let's first look at the major differences and similarities between physical and online sales.

Storefront

We talked about the importance of the physical storefront, down to the aesthetics of the parking lot.

Similarly, the optics and strategy of any virtual storefront are just as important to consider.

Just as you must do your research and narrow down where in the real world your target customer shops, if you sell your goods or services online, you must also figure out where they go in the virtual world.

There are a few large online retailers out there, but by far the biggest is Amazon. In this case, it is important to think about what Amazon customers see and how they behave. While

Amazon is the biggest online retailer in the U.S., before you list your products with them, be sure that *your* clients do, in fact, buy from them.

Listing your products with a third party creates a perception that differs from having your own website. If you cater to a niche market or offer a specialized or exclusive product, you may not benefit from a storefront that instills the idea that your products are for sale anywhere and everywhere. The idea that your own website is a specialty store; an exclusive place to purchase your unique product may make more sense. Again, it all goes back to *who* you serve.

Multiple Storefronts

If you do decide that selling through third party sites is the way to go, bear in mind the costs associated with overseeing multiple storefronts. You will need to continuously monitor the separate environments of these storefronts, managing different price points, fees and other variables. With each added storefront, the task of precisely measuring and analyzing these variables—not to mention the behavior of your sales themselves—becomes bigger and bigger.

In short, be aware of the scope, and the likelihood of scope-creep, in your entire sales process.

With keeping the whole sales process in mind comes another big factor of online sales and the major difference between virtual and physical sales: the delivery. As much as we've talked about the immediate after sale, this time frame for online purchases is make or break.

Vet your carriers and solidify your delivery mechanisms. For the sales cycle to complete successfully, you and your team need to make sure that the goods arrive on your customer's doorstep when you say they are going to arrive. This will determine the outcome of the end of the cycle and whether or not you will gain a loyal advocate.

Capturing the Senses - Online

In keeping with the idea that the online sales process can come as close as possible to the physical sales process, let's look at the way we can elicit the sensory responses we discussed a few sections earlier.

With the advent of new technologies, such as virtual reality, artificial intelligence and augmented reality, we can come very, very close to eliciting a lot of those same emotional, physical and sensory responses that we want in a physical sale. Of course, we shouldn't forget about phone support for an audible connection and even possibly video for a visual connection to customers. Putting a face to a service and a sale goes a long way in putting a customer's mind at ease. They have a sense that they can know—and therefore trust—whoever is on the other end of the transaction and that they will receive whatever it is that they have extended themselves financially to accomplish.

As I said before, the actual delivery of the goods and services is a major focus for online sales in away that is not applicable to sales at the physical storefront. Regardless of whether the exchange of funds occurs through your own personal website, a third-party vendor— whether it is a one-time purchase or a subscription model, be sure that you over-commit. Make sure the customer is very aware of how, when and in what form they're going to be receiving the deliverable. Before they ask, answer for them what is it that you're doing and how it is that they will receive the good or service they've bought virtually.

On that note, expectations are even more important for online sales because the customer is not able to see the product in the real world, not able to touch or feel it, and so they need to have even more communication about what's coming from you and what is expected of them as they move through the process.

Partner Up

All right! We've reached the final section that deals with "where" you serve and here is where we are going to think a little bit outside of the box. What I mean by that is to consider how your products and services are being presented to new prospects by your referral partners. As we discussed, referral partners come in different shapes and sizes—the most obvious being your loyal customers and clients. However, I'd like to challenge you to think about other referral channels.

One of the best ways to makes sales is through third parties that you have vetted and who have vetted you as well. Choose partners in fellow service industries or industries whose goods compliment your own. For example, if you sell a specialty item, say organic coconut sugar, then a great referral partner would be an organic or health-conscious recipe blog. Be sure to partner with companies that you trust and who trust you *and* the goods or services you offer.

Again, the above example ties in to *where* your target clients are. Think about a partner's storefront and how it might compliment your own. Consider their target clients. Would they get along with your target clients? Does the segment overlap?

A referral partner relationship will make you sales—and the quality of that relationship matters, you can't just pick anyone and everyone who comes along. This, dear entrepreneur, is when (and where!) sales are made.

WHAT YOU SERVE

"Quality" is the Word

"Progress is our most important product."

—old General Electric ad [14]

The quality of what you serve is paramount. It's number one, and it will always be, if you want to become an emerging and eventually, thriving business in your industry. Nothing beats quality. When it comes down to it, understanding your target client's wants and where your true sales channels are, are really just ways to better inform and cultivate the quality of your products and services.

It may seem apparent in your mind, or within the internal dialogue of your company, to prioritize coming up with new ways and means of production that are easier, more efficient and cost-effective, but bear in mind this thinking cuts out the most important perspective: that of your target client. This perspective is the yardstick by which to measure any product customization.

In every way, product improvement must be managed in terms of what your target client might want or need. Think: what is important to them and how can you add more value to their life? The more value you add to your product or service from your target client's perspective, the higher its quality and relevance. This quality and relevance will then lead to the continued demand for your product or service. That's the key: to understand that offering products and services of the utmost quality is never a static objective. It's always changing, always improving, always making sure that what you're offering is in line with technology, culture and the demands and needs of your target customers.

As you can tell, I believe that quality cannot be emphasized enough. It's a cornerstone. Often, entrepreneurs get tunnel vision and focus their main objectives on ways to drive down costs or eliminate waste. Certainly, those are necessary concerns, but your core purpose should be to maintain a clear vision of what you are serving—and, of course, for whom. Then, you can begin to craft value.

Get the Message Out

Using technology to deliver and to improve on the delivery of high-quality goods and services is more critical today than ever before. Do not be fooled into thinking that technology or a "high-tech" approach is a misnomer for you if you happen to be a part of a conventional or longstanding industry, such as automotives or agriculture.

There is so much to take advantage of as far as communicating to your target clients by way of social media, email lists and campaigns and machine learning. Being able to track and analyze the needs and behaviors of your market segment (or segments) through customized messaging can help you create a near-palpable anticipation for new products or new information about existing and upcoming products and services. You can leverage these analytic technologies and electronic communications to define what you are serving. In this way, you further come to know these customers as you would a best friend by discovering precisely what it is that they want. You can, if you pardon the expression, dangle the carrot in front of them because you can learn, in detail, what will motivate them.

That said, the sources you, as the business owner, use to learn about the latest tech trends will most likely be the same sources that your customers use. This means top industry blogs and news websites as well as major news and media outlets. Take the time to become involved in forums, online communities and discussions about the latest in your industry to stay ahead of the curve, innovate in alignment with market trends and demands and to help you choose the most relevant messaging language and platforms for your products or services.

Using the best and most germane technology to deliver not only your marketing but the product itself gives you the greatest opportunities to be seen, internalized and valued by your target client.

High-quality, specialized packaging: think iPhone boxes; or maybe video marketing using drone footage to promote your upcoming product will help you connect to more potential clients. You can showcase this video on your website, post it on YouTube or start sharing it or pay to market it on Facebook or other major social media or news outlets. This gets prospective customers to turn their heads and take notice of what you are doing. And, if you have chosen to continue the theme of quality throughout your entire process, as I so strongly suggest that you do, the higher the chance that they will also discern value just from the way that you present your product to them.

Intellectual Property

As the leader and the owner of your business, to take charge of "what" you serve, you've got to nail down the full scale of your product; to know it through and through and know how it is different from the other products out there. You need to be able to answer in excruciating detail the following question: what is your unique selling proposition? Or, to that end, what is it about your branding that has earned value or will gain worth just by its very exposure in the marketplace? This is what can become your intellectual property—something that, by law, only you can offer; a marketing phrase or image that only you can use.

The definition of Intellectual Property (IP) is a unique, intangible asset. There are a lot of different types of IP and these types of IP, or potential IP, can become various legal rights bestowed upon an inventor, an artist, creator— or a business owner, if a business entity is involved.

For example, thinking again in terms of goods, the owner of a car part manufacturing company can patent a specific, proprietary part of a car transmission. In turn, perhaps this same part manufacturer licenses the right to use the cutting-edge CNC machinery. Most likely, that machinery itself will need to purchase a license to use software and training manuals created by another third party.

Therefore, another key element to fully understanding and defining what you serve is to be fully aware of the IP ties that are related to your product or service. Not only will this help you gauge the trajectory of your product evolution, but also of your business itself. Indeed, having a keen understanding of the intellectual property you may need to purchase in order to run your business is all a part of the end price, the cost and the margins of your product.

Let's look at this in the real world. Pretend you are an interior decorating company. As a part of that, you stage homes. From time to time, you may want to hang original works of art inside the home. To do that, you've got to purchase a painting. Now, a painting, once fixed in a tangible means by the artist carries with it copyright—meaning the artist has privileges to their artwork and their creation, so that no one else has the authority or the ability to legally make copies and distribute that artistic work.

Many artists whose works are valued by the public, will seek copyright registration at the Library of Congress. Once this is achieved, it puts notice out there to the world that the artist of this particular work is taking ownership and that no one else has privileges to use the image in any way unless they explicitly give permission to make copies or derivative works—most likely for a fee.

At this point, if your interior decorating company decides to take this image from the internet or reprints it without permission and then hang it in your staged homes and take photographs for commercial purposes—i.e. to try to garner the attention of would-be buyers—that is considered commercial use without permission, which is an infringement of copyright.

Correspondingly, as an entrepreneur, you are already aware that you are building a brand. You are developing a reputation and, ideally, a reputation that engenders good will and conveys your particular style in the form of a trademark or logo and marketing campaign.

Registration of this mark, and the accompanying branding that is yours inherently, should absolutely be sought from the United States Trademark Office. Once an application is submitted, the Trademark Office will evaluate and make sure that your name is unique in that area of business, in this case what is called a classification. Once the application is processed and approved, any new business may not use your name, a similar name or a similarly confusing name, without your permission.

Likewise, before you launch a new brand or product and set the colors, logo, etc, make sure that you're aware of any possibility of potentially running afoul of infringing a trade dress and trade name. If you're a restaurant owner and you want to open a new chain of hamburger restaurants, you can't make the restaurant paint scheme red and yellow and use golden arches and expect to continue operating without being served a Cease and Desist.

To be sure, beyond the startup phase, after as a product is developed at its base level, over time, through customer feedback and through internal research and development, it should be improved upon. As business owners and leaders who consider entrepreneurship a lifestyle, we always strive to make what we serve better. When these improvements come along, it is very important to identify whether those enhancements are out there on the market already, and if these are changes that are deserving of patent protection.

If in fact you can show that such improvements are measurable enough to not be obvious above and beyond what's already been done and already published in other areas in the industry, and that it has present day utility—then you have a potentially patentable invention on an improvement to your existing product.

Contrary to popular belief, one does not necessarily need a groundbreaking, first of its kind, type of invention in order to be granted a patent. In fact, many of today's patents stand on the shoulders of giants and simply improve upon what is already in existence.

However, it is crucial to think of your potential IP in terms of its latent eligibility, protecting your mark or invention and avoiding infringement. You must be sure you understand that the brands and any efforts you put forth in new product lines do not potentially infringe on existing marks.

The last pillar of intellectual property that should be considered in a product, as far as what you're delivering, is what is known as a trade secret. Trade secrets are those inner workings or processes that are kept within the business, those "secrets" that do not leave the board room doors and that are kept within the business by computerized or physical means—many are even kept from most employees. Trade secrets get their value from being independently economically viable, valuable to your company and are detrimental to its health if in the hands of industry competitors.

For something to be considered a trade secret—a recipe or formula, for example—the "secret" must be documented and defined. To be sure, this type of legal protection will not be granted until you do so in explicit detail.

My point here is that in any case, to thrive in the market, you must intimately know what it is that you are serving. With this knowledge then comes the expertise to best position your product in the market. Patentable attributes are what will, at least in part, determine the essence of your brand, which brings us to *how* you serve.

HOW YOU SERVE

Tell Them How

This last chapter is about how you, the entrepreneur and the owner of your company, the band leader and conductor, explain and live "how" you aim to serve.

This book (and most likely other studies) is your chance to examine just exactly *how* you deliver your goods and services to your customer. In other words, a way to really piece together in a comprehensive way how it is that you lead your team and your company to success. Regardless of the details, this success comes through and by your leadership. This leadership starts by selling your team on your stated mission again and again, every day. They will listen and follow if you sell and lead with heart; they will listen and follow if they can see your relentless determination to build.

You now know the ins and outs of your plan to success. You will drive them forward by making it known where your target clients are—and where they go; what solutions your products or services bring and the value of their quality; how these products or services are going to reach these clients and how they, too, can get to know their new best friends—the clients; *who* it is that they serve.

Corralling a team sounds like a tall order, doesn't it? But this is the hack, the true "how": explain to them, as you have now done for yourself, the problem you are trying to solve. Because of your self-exploration, the solution and your mission are now crystallized. As the "band leader" you will inspire them to conduct their work in the way that you want them to. Beat the drum daily and keep everyone on the same page.

And for those that refuse to get on that page? You must say good-bye them. Hire slowly and fire quickly. This may indeed set an example, which is useful, but this process will also make sure that your team is not encumbered by dead weight. Those that don't fit or don't want to fit in with your company culture will only become just that: dead weight. What worse, they will most certainly detract those that could be or would be on your page without the influence of those that resist.

Remember, you've spent your blood, sweat and tears creating this business. Your team needs to be made up of those people who see the passion behind the operation and the passion in your eyes and in your actions. Treat these people well and make everyday a story that builds on prior wins. Continue telling this story and, over time, this will—at the very least to them—make your business legendary.

Show Them How

Talk—that is, the stories, monthly or quarterly reports, the daily drum beating, the recital of your mission, etc. are all parts of the first step to the "how" of service. The next step is to act.

Conspicuously being a person of action, one who is not risk-averse is important. Now, you probably are already aware, but be again forewarned that taking action tends to cause problems and may lead to failures. However, you are hopefully also aware that problems and failures are okay. Healthy, in fact, as they are the best kind of opportunities for learning. In this way, rewarding activity vs. rewarding caution and allowing everyone to learn from these kinds of mistakes will make the entire team smarter.

Bestowing authority and responsibility on your employees will give them a sense of ownership and that "skin in the game" will foster their own sense of proprietorship in your business. The passion you exude will become their own and everyone—from vendors to customers—will benefit.

The other major aspect of leading a team and demonstrating how you've set your company up to serve is to be a mentor and advisor to both your team and your clientele. Being present to lend a hand and direct their steps or taking the time to explain a complicated aspect of your service to a customer are great examples of what I mean when I say "take action" in the roles of mentor and advisor. Not only will this expose your team to some of your hard-won knowledge or put at ease and then delight an overwhelmed customer, it will bring acknowledgement to your abilities and gain you respect from all levels of the organization, solidifying your role as the leader.

It is important to epitomize the perception of you as the leader not for ego's sake, but for the welfare of your company. The stronger the leader, the tighter the ship.

Being an advisor and a mentor also means helping people to see the bigger picture: the company's position in the industry food chain, what the market landscape looks like and what the future can hold.

You Are Not Alone

As all good mentors and advisors over time will tell you, they themselves have had their own mentors and advisors. Perhaps that makes an openness to being advised and mentored by others even more critical than making sure you're open to mentoring and advising your management team and employees.

An unofficial board of advisors may be made up of your wife, husband, dear friend or maybe an affiliate in a similar situation but perhaps a different industry are all folks who you can bounce ideas and concerns off of. I believe this kind of support system is imperative. You most likely (and wisely) will add to this list your CPAs, attorneys, financial advisors and other kinds of strategists. These people will help stabilize you, bring new ideas to you and, at the end of the day, help you understand and see things that you didn't even know existed; help you understand and identify the things you didn't know that you didn't know.

There is tremendous power in being able to be open with these people and to find those folks that are willing to share their struggles, experience and triumphs. It will behoove you to come up with your own willingness to share your fears and shortcomings with them, so that they may guide you and support you. You will not always know all the answers.

Yes, being an entrepreneur is challenging. This book has covered a lot of ground and, hopefully, at this point you have a much better grasp of how to proceed and make your ideas successful. My hope is that you now feel that you are not alone; that you have a clear vision on what you want to deliver and a precise message to share with the right team. You can clearly and easily explain your "why." Your passion is now a locked-in ideal and that ideal extends into an entire lifestyle that encompasses spirituality, your family, health and the social and business aspects of your life.

Because you understand your vision so well, you also know your market and, even better, have been able to put together a crystal-clear picture of your target client. This avatar you've created is akin to your best friend—and this best friend is loyal, they tell others about your product or service and even refer those in their close inner circle directly to you.

You can now take this knowledge and aptly choose where to position your product in the marketplace. From where your clients orient geographically to how third parties interact with your sales process, you have done the work to make the most informed decisions about where you serve.

As to what you serve, after all of the aforementioned considerations, it would truly be an enormous misstep to ignore the quality of what you serve and the opportunity to drive value in everything thereafter. Remember this and keep attune to how to utilize current technology to market your product. Understand that things like intellectual property play a big role in making sure you protect and leverage any assets that help you create that value.

Although a leader, an entrepreneur is never alone. Build a team you can trust, find a solid network of advisors, attorneys and financial professionals. Most importantly, recognize that you live for challenge and that you will always need help. The lone wolf entrepreneur truly is a myth.

Best of luck on this journey and, of course, congratulations!

BIBLIOGRAPHY

1   Fernandes, Paula. (2018, February 19).
Entrepreneurship Defined: What It Means to Be
an Entrepreneur. Retrieved from https://www.
businessnewsdaily.com/7275-entrepreneurship-
defined.html

2   Braughton, Larry. (2018, April 19).
Entrepreneurship 101: the Huge Danger in Being
a Lone Wolf? Retrieved from https://yoogozi.
com/entrepreneurship-101-the-huge-danger-in-
being-a-lone-wolf/

3   Schwantes, Marcel. (2016, February 22). 25
Unique Leadership Quotes to Inspire and
Motivate. Retrieved from https://www.inc.com/
marcel-schwantes/25-unique-leadership-
quotes-to-empower-both-leaders-and-
followers.html

4   Warren Bennis. (2018, August 24). Wikiquote.
Retrieved 16:03, February 4, 2019 from https://
en.wikiquote.org/w/index.php?title=Warren_
Bennis&oldid=2454083

5   The Toyota Way. (n.d.). In Wikipedia. Retrieved
     February 5, 2019, from https://en.wikipedia.org/
     wiki/The_Toyota_Way

6   Covey, S. R. (1989). *The 7 habits of Highly Effective
     People*. Philadelphia: Running Press.

7   Hill, Napoleon. *Think and Grow Rich*. Read by
     Russ Williams. Gildan Media Corp: Audible, 2007.

8   Goudreau, Jenna. (2011, January 12). Deepak
     Chopra On Enlightened Leadership. Retrieved
     from https://www.forbes.com/sites/
     jennagoudreau/2011/01/12/deepak-chopra-
     on-enlightened-leadership-happiness-meaning-
     work-employee-engagement-president-barack-
     obama/#238cb5547e4e

9   Hunter, Rob. (2016, June 2). The pros and cons of
     creating a family culture in business. Retrieved
     from https://www.virgin.com/entrepreneur/
     pros-and-cons-creating-family-culture-
     business

10   Michele. (2015, September 12). The Rise and
     Fall of Eastman Kodak. Retrieved from http://
     nightowltrader.blogspot.com/2011/09/rise-and-
     fall-of-eastman-kodak.html

11   Gallo, Amy. (2014, October 29). The Value of
       Keeping the Right Customers. Retrieved from
       https://hbr.org/2014/10/the-value-of-keeping-
       the-right-customers

12   Bernazzani, Sophia. (2018, December 13).
       Customer Loyalty: The Ultimate Guide. Retrieved
       from https://blog.hubspot.com/service/
       customer-loyalty

13   Baer, Jay. (2014. August 9). The 8 Things Online
       Influencers Can Do For You. Retrieved from
       https://www.slideshare.net/jaybaer/8-things-
       online-influencers-can-do-for-you/3-92of_
       global_consumers_trustUGC_and

14   AdAge. (2003, September 15). Retrieved
       from https://adage.com/article/adage-
       encyclopedia/general-electric/98667/

Made in the USA
Columbia, SC
22 June 2019